THE TOP 30 GRAMMAR MISTAKES

A Do-it-Yourself Homeschooling Handbook

By Linda Beltran
The Thinking Tree Publishing Company, LLC
& Sarah Janisse Brown

Illustrations/Artwork by Tolik Trishkin
& Andrew Romanyuk

Design/Edit by Nora Marie Apple

Copyright 2018 — Do Not Copy — Dyslexie© Font by Christian Boer

TABLE OF CONTENTS:

4. Letter from the Author
6. Affect or Effect
8. All Ready or Already
10. A lot, A lot, or Allot
12. By, Buy, or Bye
14. What Do I Capitalize?
18. When Do I Use a Comma?
22. Compliment or Complement
24. Dangling Modifier
26. Fewer or Less
30. I or Me
32. Into or In To
34. It's or Its
36. Knew or New
38. Lay or Lie
40. Writing an Informal Letter
43. Writing a Formal Letter
46. Addressing an Envelope
48. Loose or Lose
50. Mr., Miss, Ms., or Mrs.
52. Apostrophes to Singular Nouns
54. Apostrophes to Possessive, Hyphenated, or Compound Nouns
58. Numbers or Numerals
62. Peak, Peek, or Pique
64. Principal or Principle
66. Run-on Sentences
68. Than or Then
70. Their, There, or They're
72. To, Too, or Two
74. Verbs in Passive Voice
78. Were, We're, or Where
80. Who or Whom
84. Your or You're

PRACTICE WORK PAGES:

87. How do I know? Practice Rules
96. Finding Verbs
98. Find Your Own 5 Rules
108. Copy-Work from Literature
138. Creative Writing Prompts
164. Write your Story

The Top 30 Grammar Mistakes

A fun way to learn how to avoid the most common mistakes in the English Language!

A NOTE FROM THE AUTHOR:

I tried to keep The Top 30 Grammar Mistakes simple and fun, which means not all of the rules will go into a lot of detail. Too many details can sometimes make things more confusing. It's our goal **NOT** to confuse you.

You are encouraged to dig deeper and research the rules as you work through 30 Grammar Mistakes. Hopefully, while working through The Top 30 Grammar Mistakes, it will spark an interest in grammar, and you'll **WANT** to know more.

We cover some of the rules but grammar rules change through time and with some of them there is so much more information. I encourage you to research the rules to get a further understanding of them. Some have an interesting history behind the rule and couldn't be covered in this book. I encourage you to dig deeper with each rule. To help you remember the rules, make up sentences, rhymes, or illustrations, and write about your findings on the opposite pages.

If you don't like using the internet to look things up, here are some titles of my favorite books on grammar and the English language that you can use while completing The Top 30 Grammar Mistakes:

The Blue Book of Grammar and Punctuation
    By: Jane Strause

The Only Grammar Book You'll Ever Need
    By: Susan Thruman

Basher Basics: Grammar
    By: Simon Basher

King Alfred's English: A History of the Language We Speak
    By: Laurie J. White

These books are suggestions; they are not required when completing the 30 Grammar Mistakes.

Another way to help you remember proper grammar is by reading books! When you are reading, try to notice the rule(s) you are learning and find them in your daily reading. For instance, when reading a sentence, notice when the words *it's* and *its* are used or when *who* and *whom* are used. Pay attention to commas and which words are capitalized. If you're really inclined, write the sentence that you found in your book pertaining to the rule in your journal!

Happy Fun-Schooling!
Linda Beltran

Come visit us at:
HOMESCHOOLING6.COM
FUNSCHOOLINGBOOKS.COM

HOW DO I KNOW WHEN TO USE "AFFECT" OR "EFFECT"?

Answer:

"Affect" with an "a" means to bring on or to cause a change. It can also mean to cause emotion or to provoke feelings.

"Effect" with an "e" means something brought about by a cause; the power to produce an outcome or achieve a result; to influence something or someone; a scientific law, hypothesis, or phenomenon.

You might be thinking, "Huh? That didn't help!" Try remembering this:

- "Affect" with an "A" is an action and is almost always a verb.
- "Effect" with an "E" is an end result and is almost always a noun.

Examples:

- The rain affected the traffic. (Affected is an action.)

- I am affected by ice cream because sugar has a strange effect on me and I act silly. (Think of it like this, "I am changed (or affected) by ice cream because the sugar influences (or effects) me and I act silly.")

- The effect of overeating sugar is not good. (The end result, or the outcome of eating lots of sugar, is not a good one because you might get cavities.)

YOUR TURN! Write a silly rhyme, sentence, or another way to help you remember this rule:

_____
_____
_____
_____
_____
_____
_____
_____
_____
_____
_____
_____

Draw an illustration to describe this rule:

HOW DO I KNOW WHEN TO USE "ALL READY" OR "ALREADY"?

Answer:

"All ready" means completely prepared. You want to emphasize that you are completely ready.

"Already" means to describe something that has happened before a certain time.

Examples:

- Albert was all ready to leave the house, but he took so long that everyone else had already gone. He had to walk to the park alone.

Remember – if you can leave the "all" out and only use the word "ready", then "all ready" is correct.

- Albert was ready to leave the house.

The sentence still makes sense.

Let's try taking the "all" out of "already" in the second half of the sentence.

- He took so long that everyone else had ready gone.

It doesn't make sense, so we need to use "already".

YOUR TURN! Write a silly rhyme, sentence, or another way to help you remember this rule:

Draw an illustration to describe this rule:

HOW DO I KNOW WHEN TO USE "ALOT", "A LOT," OR "ALLOT"?

Answer:

"Alot" is not a word. It is frequently misused, so remember when you put the "a" with the word "lot" it's wrong. Don't do that. 🙂

"A lot" means you have a vast amount.

"Allot" means to assign a certain amount or portion, or as my son would say, "Divvy it up".

Examples:

- I have a lot of cookies.
- My mom has a lot of experience baking cookies.
- My mom will allot 10 minutes to each of us to clean our room.
- I have 50 cookies and will allot 10 of them to each person. (Wow, that's a lot of cookies!)

So remember if you have a vast amount you use "a lot", but if you are distributing or divvying something up, you use "allot".

YOUR TURN! Write a silly rhyme, sentence, or another way to help you remember this rule:

Draw an illustration to describe this rule:

HOW DO I KNOW WHEN TO USE "BY", "BUY", OR "BYE"?

Answer:

"By" is a preposition and is usually used before a noun or pronoun.

"Buy" is usually used with the meaning to purchase or acquire. "Buy" can also mean to accept as true, such as: "I don't buy that." (I don't believe that.)

"Bye" or "good-bye" is an acknowledgment of parting.

Examples:

- Donnie will complete the assignment **by** Monday morning.
- Dad went to the hardware store to **buy** some nails.
- The baby waved **bye-bye**.

YOUR TURN! Write a silly rhyme, sentence, or another way to help you remember this rule:

_____
_____
_____
_____
_____
_____
_____
_____
_____
_____
_____

Draw an illustration to describe this rule:

HOW DO I KNOW WHEN TO CAPITALIZE?

Answer:

1. Capitalize the first word of every sentence.

Aa Bb Cc Dd Ee Ff

2. Capitalize Proper Nouns:
   - Specific persons and things: George W. Bush and The White House.
   - Capitalize the first person singular noun "I".
   - Specific geographical locations: Lake Erie and Africa.
   - Names of planets and celestial bodies: the Milky Way, Saturn, and Jupiter. Do NOT capitalize earth, sun, and moon UNLESS they appear in the same sentence as other planets as follows: Mars is smaller than Earth. I live on earth. Earth is not capitalized in the second sentence because no other planet is mentioned.
   - Days of the week and months, but not seasons.
   - Historical events: The Crusades and World War II.
   - Brand names: Whirlpool and Ford.
   - Names of courses: Biology 101, Economics, and Algebra (except when writing, "I'm taking a biology course in the spring.").
   - Races, nationalities, and languages: Jewish, English, African American, and Hispanic.
   - Names of religions: Christianity, Judaism, and Hindu.

Gg Hh Ii Jj Kk Ll Mm

3. Titles of relations when substituting for a family member's name:
   - Don't capitalize a family relation (aunt, uncle, grandma, etc.)

when used as a common noun. Usually, there will be a possessive pronoun (my, ours, etc.) or an article (a, an, the) before the title. "Let's visit my uncle."
- We do capitalize when we use the names as a proper noun. "Let's visit Uncle today."

Tip! If you can replace the noun (uncle) with a name (Jethro) and it doesn't sound funny, it's correct.

Examples:
- "Let's visit my uncle today." Can you replace uncle with Jethro? "Let's visit my Jethro." The substitution doesn't sound right.
- "Let's visit Uncle today." Can you replace Uncle with Jethro? "Let's visit Jethro today." The substitution sounds right, so capitalizing "Uncle" is correct in this sentence.

Nn Oo Pp Qq Rr Ss

4. The first, last, and important words in a title:
   - Usually, articles and prepositions are not capitalized. For example, Green Eggs and Ham, Ann of Green Gables (unless it's the beginning of the title as in: The Happy Hollisters).

Tt Uu Vv Ww Xx Yy Zz

5. Capitalize people's titles:
   - When the title comes before the name, it's capitalized: Mayor Don Parker, Professor Jones, or U.S. Secretary of State John Powell.
   - When the title comes after the name, it's not capitalized: Don Parker, mayor of the city of Port Hueneme.

YOUR TURN! Write a silly rhyme, sentence, or another way to help you remember this rule:

Draw an illustration to describe this rule:

LET'S TAKE AN IMAGINATION BREAK!

Gordon is the Captain of a boat, but he is the only member of the crew! Let's draw some teammates for him to help set sail, and help them paint the boat:

HOW DO I KNOW WHEN TO USE A COMMA?

Answer and Examples:

1. Use a comma to separate elements in a series:

   - Rita baked cookies, swept the floor, and washed the windows.
   - The hungry boy ate a banana, apple, and a cucumber.

2. Use a comma plus a little conjunction (such as: and, but, for, nor, or, so, yet) to connect two independent clauses:

   - Rita baked cookies, but she burned the last batch. (Remember, each clause needs a subject and a verb.)

3. Use a comma when separating coordinate adjectives. If you can add an "and" or "but" between the adjectives and it still makes sense, then you would most likely need to use the comma when separating them.

For example:

- The slender, dark-haired, kind-looking woman waved to me. Or: The slender, dark-haired, and kind-looking woman waved to me. (Both sentences make sense with or without the word "and" between the adjectives.)

- The little old lady was very kind. (You don't need a comma for this sentence because you can't add "and" or "but". You wouldn't say "the little **and** old lady was very kind" because it doesn't sound right so no comma is needed.)

4. Use a comma to set off quoted elements like this:

- "I would like to buy some chocolate," said the young girl. "How much for that one?"

5. Use commas in names, dates, and addresses:

- It snowed on December **15, 2015**.
- On Saturday, December **15, 2015**, it snowed.

6. Use a comma when an abbreviated title comes after the person's name:

- Laura Fudge, M.D.
- Paul Smith, Ph.D.
- Nancy Jones, R.N.

YOUR TURN! Write a silly rhyme, sentence, or another way to help you remember this rule:

Draw an illustration to describe this rule:

LET'S TAKE AN IMAGINATION BREAK!

Gordon is on an empty island because his boat crashed! The items he needs in order to survive are on the shore. Use your imagination to help him find his survival tools:

HOW DO I KNOW WHEN TO USE "COMPLIMENT" OR "COMPLEMENT"?

Answer:

Compliment with an "i" is used when someone is admiring or giving you a flattering remark.

Example:

- The family gave compliments to Mom for the delicious meal. (Remember, if the statement is an expression of praise, compliment has an "i".)

Answer:

Complement with an "e" means something that completes or enhances something else.

Example:

- The blue shirt complements your blue eyes. (Remember, if something completes or enhances something, complement has an "e".)

YOUR TURN! Write a silly rhyme, sentence, or another way to help you remember this rule:

Draw an illustration to describe this rule:

WHAT IS A DANGLING MODIFIER?

Answer:

When you don't describe, clarify, or give enough detail about what you are communicating, it's called a dangling modifier. It is a word or phrase that refers to something or someone that is not mentioned in the sentence. The sentence does not make a complete thought. A dangling modifier is what I like to call a "Cliff Hanger." When you leave a sentence dangling, imagine the reader is confused and hanging from a cliff.

Examples:

Incorrect:
- Having finished the assignment, the computer was turned on. (Did the computer turn itself on? No. Who turned on the computer?)

Correct:
- Having finished the assignment, Samantha turned on the computer.

Incorrect:
- Famished, the pizza was devoured. (Who devoured the pizza? Let's rewrite the sentence to give a complete thought.)

Correct:
- Famished, Ethan devoured the pizza.

Incorrect:
- Running to catch the bus, the book fell in the puddle. (Was the book running and fell in the puddle? It was obviously not running, because books can't run.)

Correct:
- Running to catch the bus, I dropped my book in a puddle. (Now the sentences make sense.)

Remember: Don't leave your audience hanging!

YOUR TURN! Write a silly rhyme, sentence, or another way to help you remember this rule:

Draw an illustration to describe this rule:

HOW DO I KNOW WHEN TO USE "FEWER" OR "LESS"?

Answer:

"Fewer" is used when discussing countable things such as rocks, glasses of water, or taffy pieces. These are things you can count.

"Less" is used when you are discussing things you don't count such as water, time, hope, or emotion. You can't count a body of water, but you can count glasses of water.

Still confused? Here's a simple way to remember:

Use "less" for singular nouns or singular mass nouns (salt, sand, flour), but use "fewer" for plural nouns. If you are able to count it, use "fewer". If it's not countable, use "less".

Examples:

- Fewer kids came to Amanda's pool party than were expected. (You can count the kids at the party, so "fewer" is correct.)

- I ate fewer cookies than my sister. (You can count the cookies my sister ate, so "fewer" is correct.)

- Desert animals consume less water than animals that live in the rainforest. (In this sentence, "less" is correct because you can't count how much water the animals are consuming.)

Here are a few more examples:

- A carrot has less water than a watermelon. (Notice you can't count water.)

- A carrot has fewer ounces of water than a watermelon. (Now the water is countable. You can count "ounces" of water but not "just" water.)

Do some research on your own! Fewer and less have an interesting history.

Find out if a grocery store's advertisement, "20 items or less", is correct or not. ☺

YOUR TURN! Write a silly rhyme, sentence, or another way to help you remember this rule:

Draw an illustration to describe this rule:

LET'S TAKE AN IMAGINATION BREAK!

Gordon met thieves! They took his hat, coat, glasses, suitcase, and other things! Please help him gain it back by using your imagination to draw new things:

HOW DO I KNOW WHEN TO USE "I" OR "ME"?

Answer:

Both "I" and "me" are pronouns. "I" is a subject pronoun and "me" is an object pronoun. When you are not sure when to use "I" or "me", try the "blank and" trick. Take the words "_____ and" out of the sentence, then reread the sentence. If it makes sense, it's correct.

Examples:

- Mom and I went to the store.

Now, take the words "<u>Mom</u> and" out of the sentence. Does it still make sense? It does because, "I went to the store." is still a complete sentence and makes sense, so "Mom and I" is correct. "I" is the subject of the sentence.

- The puppy followed Jerry and I home.

Again, let's take the words "<u>Jerry</u> and" out of the sentence. Does it still make sense? "The puppy followed I home." It does not make sense because "I home" doesn't sound right. What is the subject of the sentence? The puppy is the subject. Let's try replacing the word "I" with the word "me":

- The puppy followed <u>me</u> home.

That sounds much better. "Me" is the object of who the puppy followed home. Therefore, "The puppy followed Jerry and me home." is correct.

YOUR TURN! Write a silly rhyme, sentence, or another way to help you remember this rule:

Draw an illustration to describe this rule:

HOW DO I KNOW WHEN TO USE "INTO" OR "IN TO"?

Answer:

"Into" (one word), means toward the inside of or in the direction of. It can also mean to transform or to change. "Into" is a preposition and usually answers the question, "Where?"

"In to" are actually two words. ("In" is an adverb, and "to" is a preposition.) These two words just happen to fall next to each other in some sentences.

Examples:

"Into"
- The bird flew into the window and feathers were flying everywhere, poor bird. (The bird flew where? It flew into the window.)
- The frog turned into a handsome prince! (The frog transformed into a prince.)

"In to"
- Kate came in to get her purse. (If you ask, "Kate went into where?" You don't know, therefore, "in to" is correct. If it were written: "Kate went into the kitchen to get her purse." You know where Kate went, so now "into" would be the correct form to use.)
- Janessa came in to tell Mom the good news about the job offer. (Janessa went where? We don't know. So, again, "in to" is correct. If it were written: "Janessa went into the bedroom to tell Mom the good news about the job offer." It would be correct because this time we know where Janessa went.)

YOUR TURN! Write a silly rhyme, sentence, or another way to help you remember this rule:

Draw an illustration to describe this rule:

HOW DO I KNOW WHEN TO USE "IT'S" OR "ITS"?

Answer:

"It's" is a contraction of "it is".

"Its" is the possessive form of "it".

Example:

- It's snowing outside, so the bee stayed warm in its hive.

"It's" refers to the snow. Or we could say, "It is snowing outside."

And, "its" refers to the bee. Or we could say, "The bee stayed warm in the bee's hive."

> Remember:
> It's = It is
> Its = Refers to the object

YOUR TURN! Write a silly rhyme, sentence, or another way to help you remember this rule:

Draw an illustration to describe this rule:

HOW DO I KNOW WHEN TO USE "KNEW" OR "NEW"?

Answer:

"Knew" is the past tense of "know" which is when you have knowledge of or are aware of something.

"New" describes something that has never been used, seen, or done before.

(To help you remember, think of these two words together: knew and know. They both start with the letter "K".)

Examples:

- Joanna knew most of the answers on the test!
- Mom bought Brent a new pair of shoes.

YOUR TURN! Write a silly rhyme, sentence, or another way to help you remember this rule:

Draw an illustration to describe this rule:

HOW DO I KNOW WHEN TO USE "LAY" OR "LIE"?

Answer:

Both words position someone or something in a horizontal manner.

"Lay" means to put or to place something or someone down and requires a direct object. Someone is doing the action.

"Lie" means to be in a horizontal position and cannot have an object.

Examples:

- I will lay the baby down in the crib. (Baby is the direct object of lay.)
- Mom said I must lie down and take a nap. (Think horizontally.)
- "He maketh me lie down in green pastures." ~Psalm 23:2a (A popular verse in the Bible.)

Tip! If you can replace the word lay with "place" or "put," then the word you will want to use is lay. For example, "I will lay (or put) the baby in the crib."

YOUR TURN! Write a silly rhyme, sentence, or another way to help you remember this rule:

_____
_____
_____
_____
_____
_____
_____
_____
_____

Draw an illustration to describe this rule:

HOW DO I WRITE A FRIENDLY LETTER?

Answer:

This is how you would write a proper letter to your grandma, aunt, uncle, or best friend:

[Your First and Last Name]
[Your Street Address]
[Your City, State and Zip Code]←notice the comma after the city.

-space

[Date]
-space
-space

[Salutation] Dear Grandma,

-space
-space

[Body of the letter]
- You can write about what you are learning in school, church, and youth camp.
- Write about your favorite things.
- Write about how much you miss her/him.

-space

[Closing] Love,

[Signature] Sign your first name here.

WRITE A LETTER TO YOUR FAVORITE RELATIVE.

_____

_____

_____

_____,

_____
_____
_____
_____
_____
_____
_____
_____

_____,

WRITE A LETTER TO YOUR BEST FRIEND:

HOW DO I WRITE A FORMAL LETTER TO THE GOVERNOR? (OR OTHER IMPORTANT PEOPLE...)

Answer:

A proper letter consists of:

- Heading: On the right side of the paper, put your address and date. Do not put your name.
- Inside Address: This is where you will put the name and address of the person whom you are writing to. In a formal letter, address it to a specific person. (Mr. Long) If you don't know their name, at least put their title such as Customer Service Manager. Place four spaces below the heading.
- Salutation: Two spaces below the inside address — the most used greeting is Dear_____: followed by a colon. If you don't know the person's name, write To Whom It May Concern, or Dear Sir or Madam.

    If you know the name, use one of the following titles:

    - Mr. — a male
    - Mrs. — a married female
    - Ms. — unknown status of a female or business women
    - Miss — unmarried female
    - Dr. — for a person with the status of a doctor

    Make sure you are using the person's surname with these titles and not first names.

- Body: Two spaces below the salutation and one space between paragraphs. This is where you will write your letter.
- Closing: Two spaces below the body. Only the first word of the closing should be capitalized and punctuated with a comma.

    Examples of closings:

    Warmly,

    -or-

    Yours sincerely, ←(Notice the second word is **NOT** capitalized)

- Signature: Two spaces below the closing type your name. This will leave room between the closing and your name for an actual signature.

    Warmly,

    Linda Beltran

    Linda Beltran

FORMAL BUSINESS LETTER FORMAT

[Your Street Address]
[Your City, State & Zip Code]

[Today's Date]

[Name of Recipient (Governor or official)]
[Title of Recipient]
[Organization or Company]
[Recipient's Address]
[Recipient's City, State & Zip Code]

Dear [Name of Recipient]:

- [Short introduction paragraph, stating purpose]

- [Additional information]

- [Closing information, summary or thank you as appropriate]

Sincerely,

[Sign here for letters sent by mail or fax]

[Your Printed or Typed Name]
[Title – if applicable]

- On the next page, write your own letter to an important person using the rules you learned here.

WRITE A LETTER TO YOUR GOVERNOR:

HOW DO I ADDRESS AN ENVELOPE?

Answer:

First of all, always write neatly to make sure your letter will reach the correct destination! Your address is the **RETURN** address and is always located in the upper left corner. The postal stamp belongs in the upper right corner. The kind of stamp you will use depends on the weight of the letter, card, or package. The person you are sending the letter to is the **RECIPIENT**. The recipient's address will always go in the lower middle to the right of the envelope.

Example:

Rose Lane ←Sender's Name   →Postal Stamp
123 N. Fork Rd. ←Return Street Address
Tyler, NY 59821 ←Return City, State, Zip Code

                    Linda Smith ←Recipient's Name
                    123 Lollipop Lane ←Recipient's Street Address
                    Sunflower, TX 59078 ←Recipient's City, State, Zip Code

Now it's your turn to address an envelope! (If you don't know the postal abbreviations for all the states, now would be a good time to learn them.) Address the envelope below from you to your best friend:

LET'S TAKE AN IMAGINATION BREAK!

Gordon moved to a new town! Use your imagination to help him find his way around his new house by creating the different rooms, his new furniture, and trees in his yard. Don't forget the mailbox!

HOW DO I KNOW WHEN TO USE "LOOSE" OR "LOSE"?

Answer:

"Lose" means something was lost, misplaced, or to be defeated.

"Loose" means not tight or free from constraint.

Example:

- Did you lose the library books?
- Without the proper training, you will lose the game.
- Run, there's a moose on the loose!
- These jeans are no longer loose and baggy on me.

Tip! Lost and lose both have one "o". Moose rhymes with loose. (So run, because the moose is on the loose!)

YOUR TURN! Write a silly rhyme, sentence, or another way to help you remember this rule:

Draw an illustration to describe this rule:

HOW DO I KNOW WHEN TO USE "MR.", "MRS.", "MISS", OR "MS."?

Answer:

- "Mr." is an abbreviation for Mister, and is used to address a man. (It's super easy to remember this one.)
- "Mrs." (pronounced "Missus") is the feminine form of Mister, and is used to address a married woman.
- "Miss" is used when addressing an unmarried woman.
- "Ms." (pronounced "Mizz") is used to address a married or unmarried woman who does not wish to indicate her marital status. It can also be used as a title for a business woman.

Examples:

- Mr. & Mrs. Higgins are on their way to pick up Miss Sarah.
- Miss Parker will be your substitute teacher while Mrs. Albright is away.
- Ms. Smith is vice president of a very large company.

Remember that Mr. and Mrs. both have an "r". (To help remember that these both have an "r", think of Mr. getting married and now has "s" by his side because they "r" just right for each other.)

Tip! Use "Ms." when you are in a bind and are not sure if the woman you are addressing is single or married.

Now practice using all four of these abbreviations by writing some silly sentences to help you remember!

Draw an illustration to describe this rule:

HOW DO I KNOW WHERE TO ADD AN APOSTROPHE TO A SINGULAR NOUN?

Answer:

Singular possessive nouns and pronouns demonstrate ownership of something. An apostrophe is added before the letter "s" like this: _____'s

Examples:

- Lucy's book fell. (Who owns the book? Lucy does.)

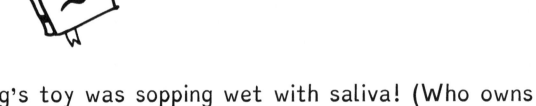

- The dog's toy was sopping wet with saliva! (Who owns the toy? The dog does.)

YOUR TURN! Write a silly rhyme, sentence, or another way to help you remember this rule:

_____
_____
_____
_____
_____
_____
_____
_____
_____
_____
_____
_____
_____

Draw an illustration to describe this rule:

WHERE DO I PUT THE APOSTROPHE USING POSSESSIVE, HYPHENATED, OR COMPOUND NOUNS?

A noun is a person, place, thing, idea, quality, or action: boy, bird, lamp, horse.

To make a singular noun possessive:
- Simply add an apostrophe and an "s" to the end of the word to show ownership: the boy's ball, the bird's nest, the lamp's shade, the horse's stall.
- When a single noun already ends in "s", just add an apostrophe: the boss' desk, the witness' testimony, the glass' handle.

To make a singular noun plural (more than one):
- Add an "s" or "es" to the end of the word: boys, birds, lamps, or horses. (Do some research to find the exceptions to this rule!)

To make a plural noun possessive:
- When a plural noun ends in "s" (like boys, birds, lamps, or horses), just add an apostrophe to the end of the word to show ownership: boys' team, babies' playpen, buses' route, or horses' barn.

For example:
- The boys' hats all looked the same. (Each boy owns a hat.)
- The boy's hats all looked the same. (One boy owns all the hats.)

Here's another example for the word horses:
- The horses' bridles were cleaned. (Each horse possesses a bridle.)
- The horse's bridles were cleaned. (One horse owns all the bridles.)

Write a sentence showing the horse owns the stall:

_____
_____
_____

Possessive plurals not ending in "s":

Some words are plural, but don't end in "s" like children, women, or sheep. In these plural words, an apostrophe + s would need to be added just like you would in a singular noun.

Example:
- The sheep's wool is soft and fuzzy. (Sheep possess the wool so it belongs to them.)
- The sheep are all in their pen. (The sheep don't own anything; therefore no apostrophe "s" is needed.

WRITE YOUR OWN SENTENCE USING THE FOLLOWING NOUNS:

bird's

lamp's

babies'

buses'

Making hyphenated nouns and compound nouns plural:

When making words possessive with hyphenated or compound words, add an apostrophe + s at the end, or at the end of the last word.
- Hyphenated example: My brother-in-law's shoes are a size **12**!
- Compound example: The bulldog's bowl is full of food.

The apostrophe + s is at the end of a proper name:
- The United States Post Office's stamps are lovely.

When two nouns are joined and ownership is separate, each noun gets their very own apostrophe + s:
- Joshua's and Caleb's rooms were freshly painted. (Joshua and Caleb each have their own room so each name gets an apostrophe.)

TIP:
··A pronoun is a word that replaces a noun in a sentence. Possessive pronouns show ownership, and therefore do not need an apostrophe:
- **His** shoes are a size **12**!
- **Their** rooms were freshly painted.

WRITE YOUR OWN SENTENCE USING THE FOLLOWING NOUNS:

dog's and cat's

great-uncle's

firefly's

Empire State Building's

LET'S TAKE AN IMAGINATION BREAK!

Gordon entered a room in his new house, but there is nothing in it! Let's draw some furniture, paintings, and pets:

HOW DO I KNOW WHEN TO WRITE OUT A NUMBER OR WHEN TO USE NUMERALS?

Answer:

Write out a number when:

- The number is at the beginning of a sentence: Twenty-five people were rescued from the sinking ship.
- The number is under ten: Tracey has two younger sisters and three older brothers.
- The number is a fraction (unless it's in a recipe, then you may use numerals): Two-thirds of the people liked chocolate ice cream over vanilla.
- When there are only a few words in a large number it's often spelled out: Two million dollars is a lot of money. (or) The company earned two million dollars.
- Time: when followed by o'clock we usually spell it out or when A.M. or P.M. is not mentioned: Mom will be home at six o'clock. (or) Mom will be home at six in the evening.

WRITE TWO SENTENCES USING THIS RULE:

_____

_____

_____

_____

_____

_____

Use numerals when:

- When writing two related numbers in a sentence: The dog moved **2** paces to the left and **12** paces to the right before finding the bone.
- When numbers are in a list it is best to keep all the numbers consistent (even if the number is lower than 9): My brothers' ages are **4, 6, 8,** and **12**.
- Dates and Years: Cora was born October **23, 2012**. (or) School begins September **10, 2015**.
- When writing percentages: In a recent survey **75%** of the people preferred chocolate chip cookies and **25%** liked snickerdoodles.

Remember: When you are not sure whether to spell or write out numbers and numerals, it's best to spell them out.

WRITE TWO SENTENCES USING THIS RULE:

_____

_____

_____

_____

_____

YOUR TURN! Write a silly rhyme, sentence, or another way to help you remember this rule:

_____
_____
_____
_____
_____
_____
_____
_____
_____
_____
_____
_____

Draw an illustration to describe this rule:

LET'S TAKE AN IMAGINATION BREAK!

Gordon bought a Christmas tree for his new house, but he has no decorations! Let's help him add lights, tinsel, and presents:

HOW DO I KNOW WHEN TO USE "PEAK", "PEEK", OR "PIQUE"?

Answer:

"Peak" is the highest point degree or volume of something. We usually think of a mountain peak.

"Peek" means to take a quick look.

"Pique" can mean to stimulate curiosity or interest, but it can also mean to feel irritated or resentful.

Examples:

- When he heard the word pizza, it piqued his interest. He peeked in the kitchen and became piqued when he found there was no pizza.
- Lisa was tempted to take a peek at her birthday present, but thankfully she resisted!
- The berries were past their peak making them very juicy.
- Reaching the peak of the mountain was a huge accomplishment for Gary.

**Remember, if something piqued your interest, you probably have questions about it. Both the words "pique" and "question" contain the letter "q".

Tip! "Peek" has a pair of "eyes" in the word.

To reach the heavens is the highest peak of all.

YOUR TURN! Write a silly rhyme, sentence, or another way to help you remember this rule:

Draw an illustration to describe this rule:

HOW DO I KNOW WHEN TO USE "PRINCIPAL" OR "PRINCIPLE"?

Answer:

"Principal" is a person with the highest authority. (Notice principal has the word "pal". Think of the principal as being your friend or your pal.)

"Principle" refers to a basic truth, law, or rule.

Example:

- The principal at Lovejoy Elementary school treated the students with kindness.
- My dad is a man of principle and good to his word.

Write two sentences using the words principal and principle:

_____
_____
_____
_____
_____

YOUR TURN! Write a silly rhyme, sentence, or another way to help you remember this rule:

Draw an illustration to describe this rule:

HOW DO I KNOW IF I USED A RUN-ON SENTENCE?

Answer:

A run-on sentence usually has two parts, both of which can stand on its own. Instead of being properly connected, both parts of the sentence have been fused together.

Examples:

- Run-on sentence: I enjoy writing poetry over the weekend, I'd write all weekend long if it wasn't for my chores.
- Correct: I enjoy writing poetry over the weekend. I'd write all weekend long if it wasn't for my chores.

Here's another example:

- Run-on sentence: I love to ride horses and I would ride horses daily if I had the time.
- Correct: I love to ride horses. I would ride horses daily if I had the time.

Don't let your sentence be a run-on, stop and put a period.

YOUR TURN! Write a silly rhyme, sentence, or another way to help you remember this rule:

_____
_____
_____
_____
_____
_____
_____
_____
_____
_____
_____

Draw an illustration to describe this rule:

HOW DO I KNOW WHEN TO USE "THAN" OR "THEN"?

Answer:

"Than" introduces comparison.

"Then" usually relates to time: after that, next, or afterward.

Examples:

- Sally walked to the end of the block and **then** turned left on her way to the market.

- Finish your dinner and **then** you may go outside and play.

- Texas is bigger **than** Maine. Alaska is bigger than Texas.

- My piece of cake is larger **than** yours.

>BIGGER<

YOUR TURN! Write a silly rhyme, sentence, or another way to help you remember this rule:

_____
_____
_____
_____
_____
_____
_____
_____
_____
_____
_____
_____
_____

Draw an illustration to describe this rule:

HOW DO I KNOW WHEN TO USE "THEIR", "THERE", OR "THEY'RE"?

Answer:

"Their" is used to show ownership or possession.

"There" is an adverb that means, "at that place". It indicates location or place.

"They're" is a contraction of "they are".

Example:

- They're riding their scooters on the path over there. (To break down the sentence: <u>They are</u> riding <u>the kid's</u> scooters on the path over <u>the hill</u>.)

Tip! Notice that "there" has the word "here" which is also a location.

YOUR TURN! Write a silly rhyme, sentence, or another way to help you remember this rule:

_____
_____
_____
_____
_____
_____
_____
_____
_____
_____
_____
_____

Draw an illustration to describe this rule:

HOW DO I KNOW WHEN TO USE "TO", "TOO", OR "TWO", ?

Answer:

- "To" is used in expressing motion or in the direction of (as in a particular location), or to indicate contact.
- "Too" means in addition to or to a higher degree (think of too much or too risky). The word "too" can sometimes be replaced with "also".
- "Two" is for the number **2**.

Examples:

- Let's go to the park. (Indicates a particular motion.)
- Mom applied medicine to little Danny's cut. (Indicates contact.)

- Billy ate too many cookies and became sick. (Too much.)
- Climbing the rocky mountain was too risky on a rainy day. (Too risky).
- I want to go too! (A synonym for "also".)

- Tony and Trudy went **to** the coffee shop, ordered **two** lattes, and were hyper because they had **too** much caffeine!

YOUR TURN! Write a silly rhyme, sentence, or another way to help you remember this rule:

_____
_____
_____
_____
_____
_____
_____
_____
_____
_____
_____

Draw an illustration to describe this rule:

VERBS: WHEN DO I USE ACTIVE OR PASSIVE VOICE?

Answer:

- The active voice of a verb tells that someone or something does the action of a sentence.

- The passive voice of a verb tells us that someone or something has an action done to them by someone or something else.

Examples:

- Lilly watered the flowers on Tuesday. (Active voice: Lilly is doing the action.)

- The flowers were watered on Tuesday by Lilly. (Passive voice: the flowers are having the action done to them.)

When writing, you want to use a more of an **active** voice style because a passive voice emphasizes the object of the action, which removes the "star" (the main person or thing) out of the spotlight of the sentence.

In other words, active voice puts the elements of a sentence in logical order: Lilly (main person) + watered (action) + the flowers (recipient of action) on Tuesday = logical order.

With the passive voice sentence, Lilly is no longer the emphasis of our sentence: The flowers (recipient of the action) were watered (action) on Tuesday by Lilly (the main person). The "main person" is at the end of the sequence and can be left off entirely: "The flowers were watered on Tuesday."

If you don't know who the main person ("the star") of the sentence is, then a passive voice sentence is fine.

- For example, "The window was smashed sometime around noon." We don't know who broke the window; therefore a passive voice sentence is fine.

RE-WRITE THE UNDERLINED SENTENCE ABOVE IN ACTIVE VOICE, AND ADD A "STAR":

_____
_____
_____
_____
_____

YOUR TURN! Write a silly rhyme, sentence, or another way to help you remember this rule:

Draw an illustration to describe this rule:

LET'S TAKE AN IMAGINATION BREAK!

Gordon bought a pizza for lunch, but the restaurant forgot the ingredients! Let's help add some yummy toppings:

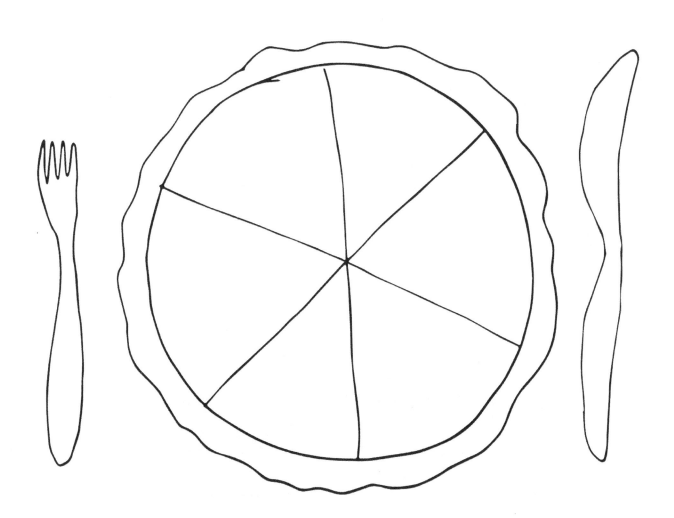

HOW DO I KNOW WHEN TO USE "WERE", "WE'RE", OR "WHERE"?

Answer:

"Were" is the past tense of "are".

"We're" is a contraction from "we are".

"Where" means "in which place" or "to which place".

Examples:

- **Where** are you going?
- **We're** going to the house for tea!
- I thought you **were** going to have hot cocoa, not tea.

Tip! Next time you can't remember whether to use where or were, remember the word "where" has an "h".

Ask, "W**h**ere are you going?"

Then answer, "To the house!"

YOUR TURN! Write a silly rhyme, sentence, or another way to help you remember this rule:

Draw an illustration to describe this rule:

HOW DO I KNOW WHEN TO USE "WHO" OR "WHOM"?

Answer:

- "Who" is a subject pronoun. It should be used to refer to the subject of the sentence. If the pronoun can be replaced with he or she, then use "who".

- "Whom" is an objective pronoun of him, her, and us, and should be used when referring to the object of the sentence. If "whom" can be replaced with him or her, then "whom" is correct.

An easier way to remember is to use the he/him test:

- he/she = who
- him/her = whom

Sometimes you may need to scramble up the words to make a statement.

Tip! Notice that "whom" ends with the letter "m" and so does the word him. Hopefully, that little test will help you remember which pronoun to use.

Examples:

- Who took my book? (Replace "who" with "he": "He took my book." The sentence still makes sense, so "who" is correct.)

- Brent is the man whom I went to the store with. (With this sentence you'll need to scramble the words to test it out, like this: I went to the store with him. You replaced "him" with "whom", and it still made sense, so using "whom" is correct.)

- Whom should I see about the job? (Should I see her/him? It makes sense so "whom" is correct.)

- Annette is the girl who received a letter. (<u>Sh</u>e received a letter vs. <u>her</u> received a letter, therefore "who" is correct.)

WRITE A SENTENCE USING "WHOM":

_____

_____

_____

WRITE A SENTENCE USING "WHO":

_____

_____

_____

YOUR TURN! Write a silly rhyme, sentence, or another way to help you remember this rule:

_____
_____
_____
_____
_____
_____
_____
_____
_____
_____
_____
_____
_____

Draw an illustration to describe this rule:

LET'S TAKE AN IMAGINATION BREAK!

Gordon picked a bouquet of flowers for his mom, but they all disappeared in the wind on his way home! Let's draw a new bouquet:

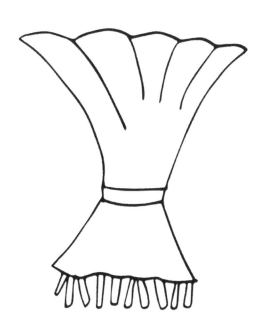

HOW DO I KNOW WHEN TO USE "YOUR" AND "YOU'RE"?

Answer:

"Your" is the possessive form of "you" and reflects ownership.

"You're" is a contraction of "you are".

Examples:

- It's time to do **your** homework!

- Please take **your** dishes to the sink.

- When **you're** done cleaning up we can go to the park.

- **You're** about to walk out the door when you notice **your** shirt is on backward!

Tip! If you can make two words out of "your" then the contraction is correct.

YOUR TURN! Write a silly rhyme, sentence, or another way to help you remember this rule:

Draw an illustration to describe this rule:

LET'S TAKE AN IMAGINATION BREAK!

Gordon is entering outer space in his space suit. What can he see in space? Let's draw some stars and planets:

HOW DO I KNOW?
(9 PRACTICE PAGES)

How do I know when to use: a colon or semicolon?

_____
_____
_____
_____
_____
_____
_____
_____
_____
_____

Draw an illustration to show what you learned:

How do I know when to use: fourth or forth?

Draw an illustration to show what you learned:

How do I know when to use: any time or anytime?

Draw an illustration to show what you learned:

How do I know when to use: assure, ensure, or insure?

Draw an illustration to show what you learned:

How do I know when to use: whether or weather?

Draw an illustration to show what you learned:

How do I know when to use: right, rite, or write?

Draw an illustration to show what you learned:

How do I know when to use: so, sew, or sow?

Draw an illustration to show what you learned:

How do I know when to use: road, rode, or rowed?

_____
_____
_____
_____
_____
_____
_____
_____
_____
_____
_____

Draw an illustration to show what you learned:

How do I know when to use: parentheses or brackets?

Draw an illustration to show what you learned:

Find and Write All 23 Helping Verbs:

In the space below, write silly sentences, a jingle, a rhyme, or a song to help you remember the helping verbs:

Find and Write the 8 State of Being Verbs:

(Practice memorizing the verbs!)

_____   _____

_____   _____

_____   _____

_____   _____

In the space below, write silly sentences, a jingle, a rhyme, or a song to help you remember the state of being verbs:
_____
_____
_____
_____
_____
_____
_____
_____
_____
_____
_____

5 RULES YOU INVESTIGATE!

Add your own grammar rule that you want to learn about:

How Do I Know When To Use _____?

_____
_____
_____
_____
_____
_____
_____
_____
_____
_____
_____

List your source for this rule:

_____
_____
_____
_____
_____
_____
_____
_____

YOUR TURN! To help you remember the grammar rule you learned; write your own silly sentence, jingle, rhyme, poem, song, or a story:

Draw an illustration to describe this rule:

YOU INVESTIGATE!

Add your own grammar rule that you want to learn about:

How Do I Know When To Use _____?

List your source for this rule:

YOUR TURN! To help you remember the grammar rule you learned; write your own silly sentence, jingle, rhyme, poem, song, or a story:

_____
_____
_____
_____
_____
_____
_____
_____
_____
_____
_____
_____
_____
_____
_____

Draw an illustration to describe this rule:

YOU INVESTIGATE!

Add your own grammar rule that you want to learn about:

How Do I Know When To Use _____?

List your source for this rule:

YOUR TURN! To help you remember the grammar rule you learned; write your own silly sentence, jingle, rhyme, poem, song, or a story:

_____
_____
_____
_____
_____
_____
_____
_____
_____
_____
_____
_____
_____
_____

Draw an illustration to describe this rule:

YOU INVESTIGATE!

Add your own grammar rule that you want to learn about:

How Do I Know When To Use _____?

_____
_____
_____
_____
_____
_____
_____
_____
_____
_____
_____
_____

List your source for this rule:

_____
_____
_____
_____
_____
_____
_____
_____
_____

YOUR TURN! To help you remember the grammar rule you learned; write your own silly sentence, jingle, rhyme, poem, song, or a story:

Draw an illustration to describe this rule:

YOU INVESTIGATE!

Add your own grammar rule that you want to learn about:

How Do I Know When To Use _____?

List your source for this rule:

YOUR TURN! To help you remember the grammar rule you learned; write your own silly sentence, jingle, rhyme, poem, song, or a story:

Draw an illustration to describe this rule:

COPY-WORK: 30 PAGES TO COPY 60 WORKS OF GREAT LITERATURE!

Research literature books at home or in the library. Find excerpts using the **30** rules and copy those paragraphs in this section.

Book Title: _____ Page Number: _____

_____
_____
_____
_____
_____
_____
_____
_____
_____
_____
_____
_____
_____

Book Title: _____ Page Number: _____

_____
_____
_____
_____
_____
_____
_____
_____
_____
_____
_____
_____
_____

Copy-work:

Book Title: _____ Page Number: ____

_____
_____
_____
_____
_____
_____
_____
_____
_____
_____
_____
_____

Book Title: _____ Page Number: ____

_____
_____
_____
_____
_____
_____
_____
_____
_____
_____
_____
_____

Copy-work:

Book Title: _____ Page Number: ____

_____
_____
_____
_____
_____
_____
_____
_____
_____
_____
_____
_____

Book Title: _____ Page Number: ____

_____
_____
_____
_____
_____
_____
_____
_____
_____
_____
_____
_____

Copy-work:

Book Title: _____ Page Number: ____

_____
_____
_____
_____
_____
_____
_____
_____
_____
_____
_____
_____
_____

Book Title: _____ Page Number: ____

_____
_____
_____
_____
_____
_____
_____
_____
_____
_____
_____
_____
_____

Copy-work:

Book Title: _____ Page Number: _____

Book Title: _____ Page Number: _____

Copy-work:

Book Title: _____ Page Number: _____

_____
_____
_____
_____
_____
_____
_____
_____
_____
_____
_____
_____
_____
_____
_____
_____

Book Title: _____ Page Number: _____

_____
_____
_____
_____
_____
_____
_____
_____
_____
_____
_____
_____
_____
_____
_____
_____

Copy-work:

Book Title: _____ Page Number: ____

_____
_____
_____
_____
_____
_____
_____
_____
_____
_____

Book Title: _____ Page Number: ____

_____
_____
_____
_____
_____
_____
_____
_____
_____
_____
_____

Copy-work:

Book Title: _____ Page Number: ____

_____
_____
_____
_____
_____
_____
_____
_____
_____
_____
_____
_____
_____
_____

Book Title: _____ Page Number: ____

_____
_____
_____
_____
_____
_____
_____
_____
_____
_____
_____
_____
_____
_____

Copy-work:

Book Title: _____ Page Number: _____

_____
_____
_____
_____
_____
_____
_____
_____
_____
_____
_____
_____
_____

Book Title: _____ Page Number: _____

_____
_____
_____
_____
_____
_____
_____
_____
_____
_____
_____
_____
_____

Copy-work:

Book Title: _____ Page Number: ____

_____
_____
_____
_____
_____
_____
_____
_____
_____
_____
_____
_____
_____
_____
_____

Book Title: _____ Page Number: ____

_____
_____
_____
_____
_____
_____
_____
_____
_____
_____
_____
_____
_____
_____
_____

Copy-work:

Book Title: _____   Page Number: ____

_____
_____
_____
_____
_____
_____
_____
_____
_____
_____

Book Title: _____   Page Number: ____

_____
_____
_____
_____
_____
_____
_____
_____
_____
_____

Copy-work:

Book Title: _____ Page Number: ____

_____
_____
_____
_____
_____
_____
_____
_____
_____
_____
_____
_____
_____

Book Title: _____ Page Number: ____

_____
_____
_____
_____
_____
_____
_____
_____
_____
_____
_____
_____
_____

Copy-work:

Book Title: _____ Page Number: _____

_____
_____
_____
_____
_____
_____
_____
_____
_____
_____

Book Title: _____ Page Number: _____

_____
_____
_____
_____
_____
_____
_____
_____
_____
_____

Copy-work:

Book Title: _____ Page Number: ____

Book Title: _____ Page Number: ____

Copy-work:

Book Title: _____ Page Number: ____

_____
_____
_____
_____
_____
_____
_____
_____
_____
_____
_____
_____

Book Title: _____ Page Number: ____

_____
_____
_____
_____
_____
_____
_____
_____
_____
_____
_____
_____

Copy-work:

Book Title: _____ Page Number: ____

_____
_____
_____
_____
_____
_____
_____
_____
_____
_____
_____
_____
_____
_____

Book Title: _____ Page Number: ____

_____
_____
_____
_____
_____
_____
_____
_____
_____
_____
_____
_____

Copy-work:

Book Title: _____ Page Number: ____

_____
_____
_____
_____
_____
_____
_____
_____
_____
_____
_____
_____
_____

Book Title: _____ Page Number: ____

_____
_____
_____
_____
_____
_____
_____
_____
_____
_____
_____
_____
_____

Copy-work:

Book Title: _____ Page Number: ____

_____
_____
_____
_____
_____
_____
_____
_____
_____
_____
_____
_____
_____
_____
_____

Book Title: _____ Page Number: ____

_____
_____
_____
_____
_____
_____
_____
_____
_____
_____
_____
_____
_____
_____
_____

Copy-work:

Book Title: _____   Page Number: ____

_____
_____
_____
_____
_____
_____
_____
_____
_____
_____

Book Title: _____   Page Number: ____

_____
_____
_____
_____
_____
_____
_____
_____
_____
_____

Copy-work:

Book Title: _____ Page Number: ____

Book Title: _____ Page Number: ____

Copy-work:

Book Title: _____ Page Number: _____

_____
_____
_____
_____
_____
_____
_____
_____
_____
_____
_____
_____

Book Title: _____ Page Number: _____

_____
_____
_____
_____
_____
_____
_____
_____
_____
_____
_____
_____

Copy-work:

Book Title: _____ Page Number: _____

_____
_____
_____
_____
_____
_____
_____
_____
_____
_____
_____
_____
_____
_____
_____

Book Title: _____ Page Number: _____

_____
_____
_____
_____
_____
_____
_____
_____
_____
_____
_____
_____

Copy-work:

Book Title: _____   Page Number: ____

Book Title: _____   Page Number: ____

Copy-work:

Book Title: _____ Page Number: ____

_____
_____
_____
_____
_____
_____
_____
_____
_____
_____
_____
_____
_____

Book Title: _____ Page Number: ____

_____
_____
_____
_____
_____
_____
_____
_____
_____
_____
_____
_____
_____

Copy-work:

Book Title: _____ Page Number: ____

_____
_____
_____
_____
_____
_____
_____
_____
_____
_____
_____
_____
_____
_____
_____

Book Title: _____ Page Number: ____

_____
_____
_____
_____
_____
_____
_____
_____
_____
_____
_____
_____
_____
_____
_____

Copy-work:

Book Title: _____ Page Number: ____

_____
_____
_____
_____
_____
_____
_____
_____
_____
_____
_____
_____
_____

Book Title: _____ Page Number: ____

_____
_____
_____
_____
_____
_____
_____
_____
_____
_____
_____
_____
_____

Copy-work:

Book Title: _____ Page Number: ____

_____
_____
_____
_____
_____
_____
_____
_____
_____
_____
_____
_____
_____

Book Title: _____ Page Number: ____

_____
_____
_____
_____
_____
_____
_____
_____
_____
_____
_____
_____
_____

Copy-work:

Book Title: _____ Page Number: ____

_____
_____
_____
_____
_____
_____
_____
_____
_____
_____
_____
_____
_____
_____
_____

Book Title: _____ Page Number: ____

_____
_____
_____
_____
_____
_____
_____
_____
_____
_____
_____
_____
_____
_____
_____

Copy-work:

Book Title: _____ Page Number: ____

_____
_____
_____
_____
_____
_____
_____
_____
_____
_____
_____
_____

Book Title: _____ Page Number: ____

_____
_____
_____
_____
_____
_____
_____
_____
_____
_____
_____
_____
_____

Copy-work:

Book Title: _____ Page Number: ____

_____
_____
_____
_____
_____
_____
_____
_____
_____
_____
_____
_____
_____
_____
_____

Book Title: _____ Page Number: ____

_____
_____
_____
_____
_____
_____
_____
_____
_____
_____
_____
_____
_____
_____

29 CREATIVE WRITING PAGES: USING YOUR GRAMMAR KNOWLEDGE

Using this picture as your writing prompt, write a story using one or more of the 30 grammar rules:

Title: _____ Rule: _____

Using this picture as your writing prompt, write a story using one or more of the 30 grammar rules:

Title: _____ Rule: _____

Using this picture as your writing prompt, write a story using one or more of the 30 grammar rules:

Title: _____ Rule: _____

Using this picture as your writing prompt, write a story using one or more of the 30 grammar rules:

Title: _____ Rule: _____

Using this picture as your writing prompt, write a story using one or more of the 30 grammar rules:

Title: _____ Rule: _____

Using this picture as your writing prompt, write a story using one or more of the 30 grammar rules:

Title: _____ Rule: _____

Using this picture as your writing prompt, write a story using one or more of the **30** grammar rules:

Title: _____ Rule: _____

Using this picture as your writing prompt, write a story using one or more of the **30** grammar rules:

Title: _____ Rule: _____

Using this picture as your writing prompt, write a story using one or more of the **30** grammar rules:

Title: _____ Rule: _____

Using this picture as your writing prompt, write a story using one or more of the 30 grammar rules:

Title: _____ Rule: _____

Using this picture as your writing prompt, write a story using one or more of the **30** grammar rules:

Title: _____ Rule: _____

Using this picture as your writing prompt, write a story using one or more of the 30 grammar rules:

Title: _____ Rule: _____

Using this picture as your writing prompt, write a story using one or more of the 30 grammar rules:

Title: _____ Rule: _____

WRITE YOUR OWN STORY OR SHORT STORIES!

Title: _____

Title: _____

Title: _____

Title: _____

Title: _____

Title: _____

Title: _____

Title: _____

Title: _____

Title: _____

Title: _____

Title: _____

Title: _____

Title: _____

Title: _____

Title: _____

Made in the USA
Columbia, SC
27 September 2018